DESTINATION JUPITER

GILES SPARROW

PowerKiDS
press

New York

Published in 2010 by The Rosen Publishing Group
29 East 21st Street, New York, NY 10010

U.S. Editor: Kara Murray

Picture Credits
Key: t – top, b – below, c – center, l – left, r – right. iStockphoto: Jane
Norton 14; NASA: 2, 2-3, 4r, 6, 7, 8t, 12-13, 18b, 26l, 27, 29, Michael
Carroll 26b, HST 28b, JPL TP, 8b, 11c, 11b, 14-15, 16-17, 19t, 20t, 20b,
21t, 21b, 22, 23t, 23b, 24t, 24c, Lowell Observatory/John Spencer 18-19;
Photos.com: 10, 25b; Science Photo Library: Julian Baum 28t, Christian
Darkin 22cl, Victor Habbick Visions 9; Shutterstock: Broukoid 6-7,
George Toubalis 4c

Front cover: NASA: bl, JPL c; Back cover: NASA: JPL; Backgrounds: NASA

Special thanks to Science Photo Library

Library of Congress Cataloging-in-Publication Data

Sparrow, Giles.
  Destination Jupiter / Giles Sparrow. — 1st ed.
      p. cm. — (Destination solar system)
  Includes index.
  ISBN 978-1-4358-3444-6 (lib. bdg.) — ISBN 978-1-4358-3487-3 (pbk.) —
ISBN 978-1-4358-3488-0 (6-pack)
  1. Jupiter (Planet)—Juvenile literature. I. Title.
  QB661.S659 2010
  523.45—dc22

                                              2008053824

Manufactured in China

CONTENTS

>>>>>>> **CONTENTS** >>>>>>>

WHERE IS JUPITER?

Jupiter is the fifth planet from the Sun. It is the largest planet in the **solar system**. It is so big that all the other planets put together could fit inside it.

Like all the planets in the solar system, Jupiter moves around the Sun following a nearly circular path, called an **orbit**. Jupiter orbits about 483 million miles (777 million km) from the Sun—as far as you would travel if you flew around Earth 20,000 times.

The time it takes for a planet to complete one orbit is the length of its year. Because

SIZE COMPARED TO EARTH

Jupiter's diameter: 88,846 miles (142,984 km)

Earth's diameter: 7,926 miles (12,756 km)

DISTANCE FROM THE SUN

Jupiter is the fifth planet and the first of the giant outer planets. They are made mostly of gas. The four inner planets are made of rock. The dwarf planet Pluto is made of ice.

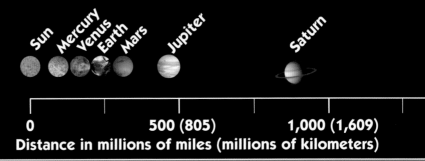

Sun Mercury Venus Earth Mars Jupiter Saturn

| 0 | 500 (805) | 1,000 (1,609) |

Distance in millions of miles (millions of kilometers)

The solar system is made up of the Sun, the planets, and the asteroid belt, a ring of rocks that orbit between Jupiter and Mars.

upiter is much farther from the Sun han Earth, its orbit is also longer. One year on Jupiter lasts 4,329 Earth days—nearly 12 Earth years.

magine you are about to go on a **mission** to Jupiter. The distance between Earth and Jupiter is continually changing as the two planets move around the Sun. You will leave when Earth is closest to upiter, as the planets line up on the ame side of the Sun.

Getting to Jupiter

The time it takes to reach Jupiter depends on how you travel, and on the positions of Jupiter and Earth in their orbits when you set off.

Distance from Earth to Jupiter	
Closest	367 million miles (591 million km)
Farthest	600 million miles (966 million km)

By car at 70 miles per hour (113 km/h)	
Closest	600 years
Farthest	1,000 years

By rocket at 7 miles per second (11 km/s)	
Closest	607 days
Farthest	992 days

Time for radio signals to reach Mars (at the speed of light)	
Closest	33 minutes
Farthest	54 minutes

Uranus

Neptune

Pluto

2,000 (3,219)   2,500 (4,023)   3,000 (4,828)   3,500 (5,633)

ON THE WAY

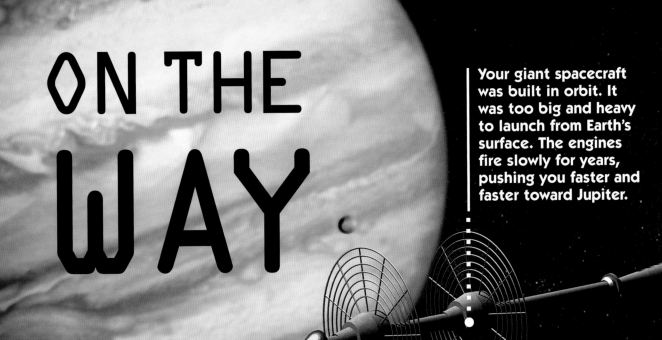

Your giant spacecraft was built in orbit. It was too big and heavy to launch from Earth's surface. The engines fire slowly for years, pushing you faster and faster toward Jupiter.

It is your last night on Earth for a long time. In the dark sky, you can see what looks like a large, yellow star. That is Jupiter, a giant world that will take five years to reach.

A LONG WAY TO GO

It is time to set off. You have a long way to go. As the ship heads off, Earth and the Moon get smaller in the window. Then there is nothing much to see. After about a year you cross the orbit of Mars and then the **asteroid** belt.

It is another four years before you reach the Jupiter system. In that time the yellow blob of Jupiter has grown gradually brighter. The planet fills the window of your spacecraft, and four bright moons—each as big as small planets themselves—are easy to spot.

STRIPES AND SPOTS

You can also see details on Jupiter's wide face: brown and cream stripes and a big red spot. By watching the spot disappear and reappear as the planet **rotates**, you can time the length of Jupiter's day. It is only 10 hours long! Despite being the solar system's largest planet, Jupiter's day is the shortest.

FLICKERS AND SHADOWS

Jupiter's moons are visible as disks, dwarfed by the planet they orbit. One moon has cast a tiny shadow on Jupiter's face. You also notice flashes of light on Jupiter's dark side and shining rings of light at the **poles**. Like Earth, Jupiter has lightning and **auroras**, better known as northern and southern lights. Finally, the rocket engines turn off and the ship becomes silent. You are now floating in zero **gravity**, in orbit above Jupiter.

The first leg of your journey to Jupiter was made on a space shuttle, which took you to a much larger spacecraft in orbit.

IN THE CLOUDS

Jupiter's clouds are very different from those of Earth. They are not a thin covering over a rocky world below, but just the top layer in a ball of gas thousands of miles (km) deep.

SWIRLING GAS

The largest features on Jupiter are wide bands of clouds that give it a striped appearance. After watching for a while, you notice that some bands appear to be moving backward compared to their neighbors. The boundaries between the bands look rough, with ripples and whirlpools where the clouds mix together.

CLOUD LAYERS

Flying in for a closer look, you glide over the cloud tops and find that the upper clouds are nearly all cream colored. You can see other colors where holes in the top layer allow you to see down to the deeper cloud layers below.

This picture shows Jupiter's north pole, so the cloud bands look like rings.

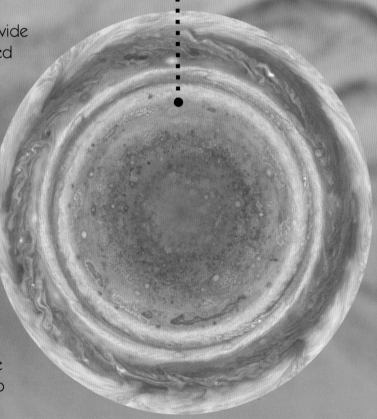

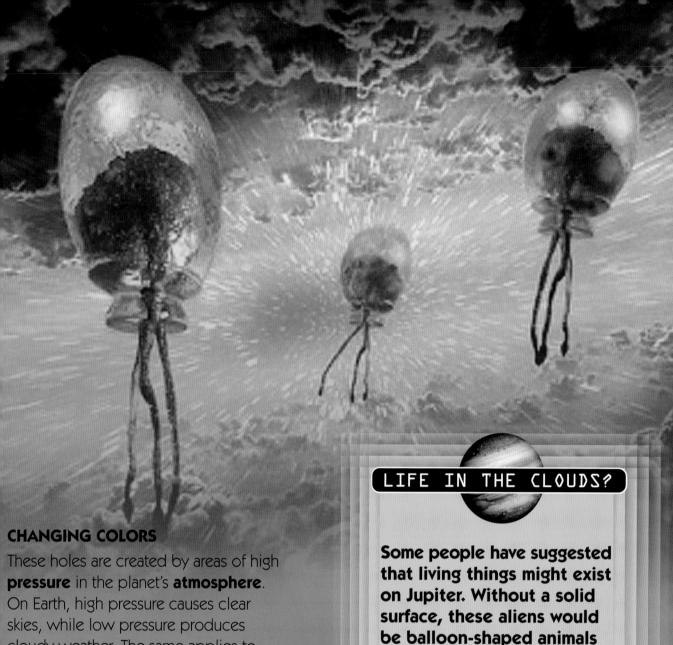

CHANGING COLORS

These holes are created by areas of high **pressure** in the planet's **atmosphere**. On Earth, high pressure causes clear skies, while low pressure produces cloudy weather. The same applies to Jupiter, but here the high pressure just creates gaps in the upper clouds rather than completely clear skies.

Brown and cream are the most common cloud colors. The deeper clouds are blue, while the ones at the very top of the atmosphere are red. Jupiter's atmosphere gets hotter as it gets deeper—blue clouds are warmest, while the red ones are cold.

LIFE IN THE CLOUDS?

Some people have suggested that living things might exist on Jupiter. Without a solid surface, these aliens would be balloon-shaped animals (above) that floated in the planet's clouds. However, space probes have shown that Jupiter's atmosphere does not have the chemicals needed for life, but balloon creatures might still live elsewhere in the universe!

THE GREAT RED SPOT

Jupiter's clouds have inside them a giant storm larger than two Earths. Welcome to the Great Red Spot.

ENDLESS STORM

Like a hurricane on Earth, the Great Red Spot spins around, sucking clouds into a vast whirlpool and producing ferocious winds. However, in other ways the spot is very different from a hurricane. As well as being much bigger and having faster winds, it never dies away. The Great Red Spot has been seen for hundreds of years, and although it changes color and fades from time to time, the storm system shows no sign of ever ending.

The Great Red Spot is the largest storm in Jupiter's atmosphere. It is about 16,000 miles (25,750 km) wide—more than twice Earth's width.

Astronomers are beginning to understand how the storms on Jupiter last for hundreds of years. By modeling clouds in a laboratory, astronomers have shown that spinning areas in a gas giant's atmosphere tend to merge to form a single, larger storm. In 1998, the *Galileo* spacecraft saw two swirls (below) that later merged to form a single, giant storm.

The Great Red Spot has different cloud levels. The highest are red and white, the lowest are blue and black.

RED BULGE

The Great Red Spot sticks out above the rest of the atmosphere, forming a bulge that is 5 miles (8 km) higher than the cream clouds around it.

From your orbit, you can see that the spot "eats" other weather systems. As you watch, white clouds the size of North America drift towards the spot and are swept up by the 250 mile per hour (400 km/h) winds. Within minutes the smaller storms are swallowed.

HUNGRY SWIRL

The Great Red Spot turns counterclockwise, taking about seven days to make one complete spin. It is always in the middle of the southern **hemisphere**, but it does not stay in the same place. It races around Jupiter faster than the planet rotates and catches up with other storms before swallowing them.

WHAT IS INSIDE JUPITER?

You cannot land on Jupiter because it does not have a solid surface. You could take a trip into the planet, but you would never come back!

DEADLY FLIGHT

Trapped by Jupiter's huge gravity, your spacecraft would keep falling until the enormous pressure of the atmosphere crushed the craft and everything inside it —including the crew.

GAS AND LIQUID

Jupiter is mostly **hydrogen**—the most common **element** in the universe. In the upper region of the atmosphere the hydrogen is mixed with other chemicals, and these form Jupiter's clouds. The cloud layer extends only a short way into the planet—about 50 miles (80 km). Below it is a calmer inner region of hydrogen air, and below this is an ocean of liquid hydrogen and **helium** extending about a tenth of the way to the planet's center, or **core**. This strange ocean has no surface like on Earth. Instead, it merges gradually into the air above.

One of the few spacecraft to make the one-way trip into Jupiter was the *Galileo* spacecraft, which burned up among the thick clouds in 2003.

LIQUID CENTER

The **temperature** and pressure rise steadily inside Jupiter as the hydrogen is squeezed ever tighter by gravity. Toward the bottom of the ocean, strange things start to happen. The hydrogen **atoms** act like liquid metal. Jupiter's fast rotation makes the **metallic hydrogen** spin, and that creates an immense **magnetic field** around the planet. Jupiter's field is 20,000 times more powerful than Earth's.

No one knows what Jupiter's core is made of. It might be a ball of rock or hot ice several times bigger than Earth or perhaps the liquid hydrogen goes all the way to the center.

hydrogen air

hydrogen and helium ocean

metallic hydrogen

core

The core of Jupiter is hotter than the surface of the Sun.

A DAY ON
JUPITER

You cannot take a walk on Jupiter's surface, but you want to see more of the planet. You fly into the clouds, suit up, and take a walk on the ship's roof.

COLD AND DARK

The first thing you notice is how heavy you feel—more than twice as much as you do on Earth! With a thick spacesuit on, it is very difficult to stand up!

Jupiter rotates once every 9 hours 55 minutes. At dawn, the Sun rises quickly above the horizon, but because it is so far away the rays are very weak. The cloud tops are a freezing −166°F (−110°C).

Earth's lightning is dwarfed by that on Jupiter, where lightning bolts are 12,500 miles (20,000 km) long.

The cloud bands near the equator rotate faster than those near the poles. As a result, Jupiter's cloud pattern is always changing.

As night falls you see colors in the sky —an aurora. This is caused by **charged particles** that get trapped by Jupiter's magnetic field and smash into the atmosphere, making air **molecules** glow.

WEATHER REPORT

On your tour through the cloud layer, the weather keeps changing. Jupiter has torrential rain, blizzards of snow, screaming winds, tall thunderstorms, and lightning bolts hundreds of times more powerful than any on Earth.

As well as stormy weather, Jupiter has hot spots. These are high-pressure areas where creamy clouds disappear to reveal blue clouds below. As you fly into a hot spot, your spacecraft shakes as you come out from a storm cloud into a sunny, calm area, with warmth rising from deep within the planet.

CLOUD FORMATIONS

Clouds on Jupiter form in a similar way to those on Earth, but they are made of many different chemicals.

High in the atmosphere, the hydrogen air gets very cold. The gases turn into droplets or freeze into ice crystals, which float as clouds.

Scientists can tell what other chemicals are in a cloud by looking at its temperature and color. For example, the yellow clouds have sulfur in them.

HOW JUPITER FORMED

As a gas giant, Jupiter formed in different conditions to those of the rocky planets, such as Earth.

Most of the gas cloud that surrounded the young Sun ended up becoming part of Jupiter. The other planets formed from the leftovers.

BORN IN A CLOUD

All the planets were born about 4.5 billion years ago, shortly after the Sun itself started shining. The Sun formed from a huge cloud of gas, ice, and dust. The remains formed a disk of **debris** around the Sun. Clumps formed in the debris, which gradually stuck together until they grew into planets.

TWO IDEAS

It is possible that Jupiter formed around a solid core of ice and dust about the size of Earth. The core's gravity would have pulled in the gases that now make up most of the planet. Another idea is that Jupiter formed entirely from a ball of gas that got smaller under the pull of its own gravity.

ALMOST A STAR

Jupiter is as big as a planet can get. If more material were added, it would not get much wider, it would just get **denser**. Jupiter is made from the same ingredients as the Sun, but it is not dense enough to burn. Jupiter would need to weigh about 80 times more to turn into a star. It is more like a **brown dwarf**, an object about 12 times heavier than Jupiter, which shines dimly because of the heat inside.

Jupiter has a faint ring system. It is made from the dust left over as Jupiter formed.

The ring system has three parts. The main ring stretches thousands of miles (km) into space but is only a few miles (km) thick. Wrapped around this like a sandwich are the faint gossamer rings. Closest to Jupiter is the halo ring, which is 12,000 miles (19,300 km) thick. That is wider than Earth.

The dust in the main ring is pulled into Jupiter by the magnetic field. However, the rings are refilled as moons inside the ring system are hit by meteorites. That lets dust clouds out into the rings.

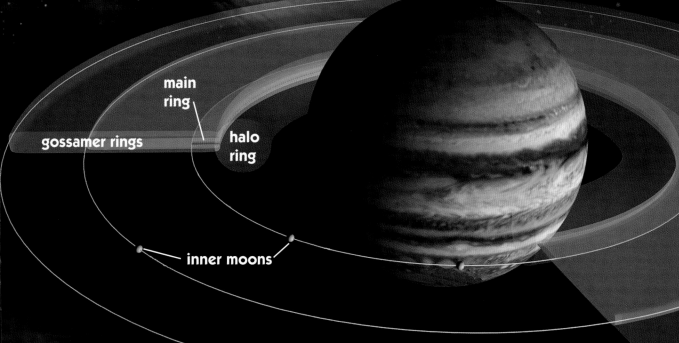

main ring

gossamer rings

halo ring

inner moons

THE JUPITER SYSTEM

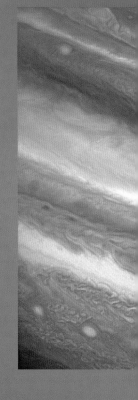

Jupiter is a giant planet and has a huge family of moons. It is almost like a smaller solar system.

INNER MOONS

Jupiter has 63 Jovian moons. Sixteen of them have names, the rest are numbered. Closest in are four tiny moons that orbit inside Jupiter's rings: Metis, Adrastea, Amalthea, and Thebe.

Then come the four largest moons, each thousands of miles (km) across. These are Io, Europa, Ganymede, and Callisto. They are named the Galilean moons because they were discovered by the astronomer Galileo Galilei in the seventeenth century.

OUTER MOONS

Some 7 million miles (11 million km) from Jupiter is the third group: Leda, Himalia, Lysithea, and Elara. These small moons, a few miles (km) across, have tilted orbits around Jupiter.

Finally, 14 million miles (23 million km) out is the last group: Ananke, Carme, Pasiphae, and Sinope. Unlike the other moons, they orbit the planet in a clockwise direction.

Adrastea   Th

Metis   Amal

Distance in thousands of miles (km)	75 (120)	100 (160)	125 (200)

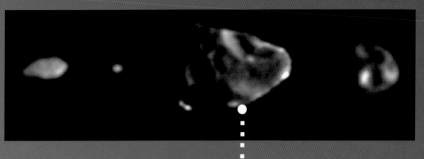

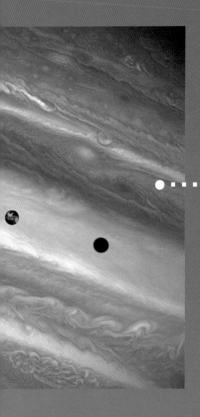

Io looks tiny orbiting above Jupiter, casting a small shadow on the planet's clouds. Nevertheless, Io is larger than our Moon.

Metis, Adrastea, Amalthea, and Thebe are shown to scale from left to right. Thebe (far right) is about 60 miles (100 km) wide.

ROCK AND ICE

The inner eight moons are a mix of rock and ice similar to what might form the core of Jupiter. The moons probably formed from material left over by Jupiter. The Galilean moons are so large because they formed where the dust and ice was thickest.

The eight outer moons are probably asteroids captured by Jupiter's gravity. This explains the odd orbits of these moons and why they look so different from each other.

Most of Jupiter's moons are just large lumps of rock, but the Galilean moons are little worlds in their own right.

Io
Ganymede
Europa
Callisto

Leda
Lysithea
Himalia
Elara

Ananke

Pasiphae
Carme
Sinope

All the moons are named for characters in Greek legends.

00	600	900	1,200	6,500	7,500	13,000	13,500	14,000	14,500
80)	(970)	(1,450)	(1,930)	(10,500)	(12,000)	(20,900)	(21,700)	(22,500)	(23,300)

GALILEO'S MOONS

It is time to take a look at Jupiter's main moons. If these worlds were orbiting the Sun instead of Jupiter, we would call them planets instead of moons.

The surface of Io is always changing as lava floods from volcanoes.

FIRST STOP

You steer your ship toward Io, the nearest Galilean moon. You can see a faint cloud of dust around Io as you make the final approach for landing.

Io has almost no air, so the sky is always black and starry. The moon keeps the same face locked toward Jupiter all the time, so the giant planet hangs in the sky all day. It is about 40 times the size of a full moon on Earth.

Io's metal core is surrounded by a thick mantle of molten rock that extends nearly all the way to the surface.

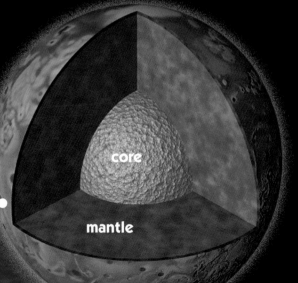

core

mantle

LAND OF VOLCANOES

Now you can see where that dust comes from. There is a giant fountain shooting hundreds of miles (km) up. It is a **geyser**, a jet of boiling liquid from underground. As well as geysers, there are thousands of volcanoes on the moon. Io is the most volcanically active world in the solar system. It is continually replacing its surface, coloring it with spots of yellow, brown, and black **sulfur**.

WATER MOON

Europa is the next stop. From space it looks bluish white, with hundreds of pink scratches. You will see why when you land. Europa is completely covered with ice.

You land in an area covered with ridges. Suddenly the ground shakes. A blast of steam shoots up before dying away in a shower of snowflakes. Europa's ice keeps cracking and refreezing. This explains the long lines of ridges.

core

rock

water

Europa's metallic core is covered by a layer of rock. Around this is a deep layer of water, which may be either frozen or liquid. The crust is made of rock-solid ice.

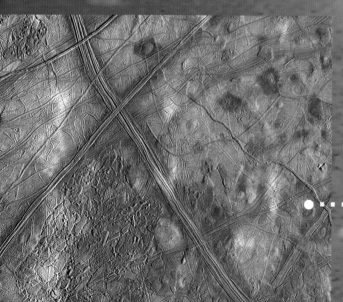

The ridges that cover Europa form as the ice crust moves. That suggests that liquid water is churning away under the surface.

LIFE ON EUROPA?

In the deepest and coldest parts of Earth's oceans, life exists around warm volcanic vents, or black smokers. They let out chemicals that are eaten by bacteria and animals. Some scientists think that alien life (below) might exist around sulfur vents in Europa's oceans.

The heat from undersea volcanoes creates currents in Europa's hidden ocean. These currents crack the moon's icy crust and force out jets of water.

HEAT FROM JUPITER

The idea that one of Jupiter's moons could have liquid water might seem impossible in such a cold place. Astronomers think that the tug of Jupiter's gravity heats Io's **mantle** so much the rocks melt. The same force could do the same to Europa. Volcanic eruptions deep inside the moon would melt the ice and create a warm ocean beneath the icy **crust**.

Perhaps Europa started out with a thick crust of ice and melted from the inside out. Its ocean might be as much as 100 miles (160 km) deep.

Where the moon's frozen surface cracks apart, water from the inside bubbles to the surface. It then freezes, resealing the crack and protecting the inside.

undersea volcano

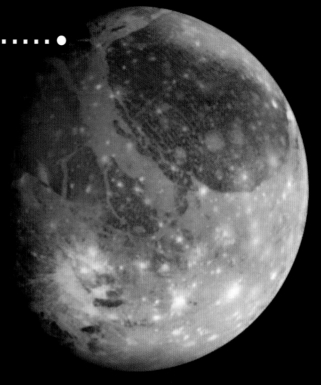

Ganymede's craters are white, which suggests that there is ice under the surface.

GIANT MOON

Ganymede is the largest moon in the solar system. It is even bigger than the planet Mercury! As you fly past, you notice that the moon has two different types of surface: dark areas peppered with **craters** and paler regions covered by ridges and valleys, but few craters.

NEW SURFACE

Astronomers think the dark parts of Ganymede are rocky areas that have not changed for billions of years. That is why they have so many craters. The pale regions must be newer because they have been hit by only a few **meteorites**.

The pale regions are probably made of ice that has welled up from deep inside the moon. Below Ganymede's surface is a shifting layer of ice warmed by heat from the core. As the ice circulates inside the moon, the surface of the paler regions stretches, forming ridges and valleys. Nobody knows whether this process is still happening, or whether Ganymede has now frozen solid.

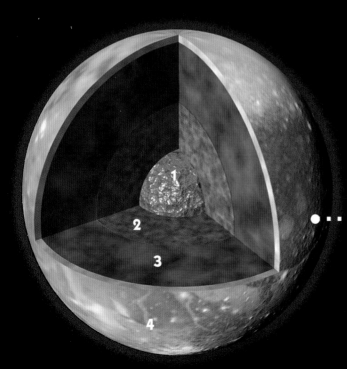

Ganymede has four layers: an inner core of iron (1), an outer core of rock and iron (2), a deep layer of warm, soft ice (3), and a solid crust of ice (4).

DARK WORLD

The outermost Galilean moon is a dark world covered in brilliant white craters. Unlike the other moons, Callisto never got hot enough to melt, but astronomers think there must be some liquid inside.

Callisto picks up magnetism from Jupiter, just like paper clips can pick up magnetism from a strong magnet. A solid moon would not do this, so scientists think that Callisto might have a hidden underground sea. They think that the water is anywhere between 6 and 60 miles (10 to 100 km) deep.

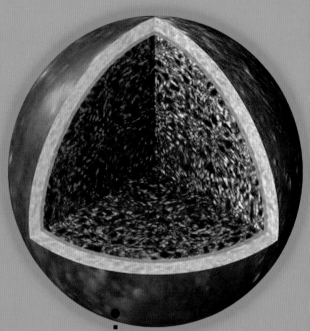

Callisto has no core. Most of the moon's inside consists of a mix of rock and ice. The crust is made of ice. Astronomers think there might also be an ocean (blue) below the crust.

Ice has been sprayed out from a bright crater (top) on Callisto. This crater is in a much larger and older one that looks gray. The ripples formed by the impact can be seen spreading out.

ICE CRATERS

A sea might also explain Callisto's bright craters. If the impact of a meteorite is strong enough to gouge through Callisto's outer rocks, then water and ice from inside can well up to the surface and freeze over to heal the gap. The bright centers of the craters are called **palimpsests**. The largest is in Valhalla, a crater the size of Arizona. The collision that produced the Valhalla crater was so strong that it left ripples stretching halfway across Callisto's surface.

LOOKING AT JUPITER

People have been looking at Jupiter for **millenia**. They followed it through the sky but had no idea what it was until about 400 years ago.

FIT FOR A KING

The Romans named Jupiter after their king of the gods. They saw the planet as a bright but slow-moving light in the sky. The first person to get a good look at Jupiter was Galileo, when he looked at the planet with a telescope in 1610.

Galileo's discoveries changed the world. In the 1600s, most people believed that Earth was the center of the universe, and everything, including the Sun, orbited around Earth. Galileo's discovery of moons orbiting Jupiter showed for the first time that some things did not go around Earth.

The Italian scientist **Galileo Galilei** studied the planets with a homemade telescope.

Jupiter was the most powerful Roman god. He was the god of the sky and controlled lightning.

A probe that might visit Jupiter soon is *Europa Explorer* (below). This orbiter will looks for Europa's hidden ocean and search for landing sites. Scientists hope to send a lander to drill through the moon's ice and explore the underground seas looking for signs of life.

EXPLORERS ARRIVE

The first **probes** to visit Jupiter were *Pioneer 10* and *Pioneer 11* in 1973 and 1974. These **NASA** probes flew to Jupiter in less than two years and returned the first photos of the planet as they flew past.

Voyager 1 and *Voyager 2* followed in 1979. These probes had better cameras and sent back close-ups of the complex cloud systems on Jupiter. The probes also were the first to look at the large moons. They discovered the icy surface of Europa, volcanoes on Io, and Jupiter's ring system.

In this artist's impression the *Galileo* orbiter passes Amalthea, Jupiter's third moon.

An artist's impression of the *Galileo* orbiter parachuting a probe into the thick clouds of Jupiter.

GALILEO VISITS JUPITER

The *Voyager* probes made short visits to Jupiter—both went on to visit more distant planets. However, astronomers wanted a longer and more detailed look at Jupiter and its moons. In 1989, *Galileo* was launched on a slow journey that would place it in orbit around Jupiter.

The *Galileo* mission had two parts: an orbiting spacecraft and an atmospheric probe made to plunge into Jupiter's atmosphere to study the conditions there. After the probe lost contact—it was crushed by the atmosphere—the orbiter began its work.

ENDING IN FIRE

The *Galileo* orbiter flew over Jupiter's clouds and passed close to the moons. The mission changed our understanding of the Jupiter system. The orbiter worked until 2003, when it fell into Jupiter's atmosphere and burned up.

COLLISION COURSE

While *Galileo* was still on its way to Jupiter, astronomers got the chance to see a **comet** crash into the planet.

The comet that smashed into Jupiter was called Shoemaker-Levy 9. It was discovered in 1993 and was actually 21 separate comets strung out in a line, rather than a single ball of ice. It was racing headlong toward Jupiter.

Before it hit Jupiter, the Shoemaker-Levy 9 comet was ripped into chunks by the planet's gravity.

The comet impact left dark marks in Jupiter's clouds that were larger than Earth itself.

COMET CRASH

Discovering the comet crash was an amazing stroke of luck because it gave astronomers a chance to study Jupiter's inside since the lumps of comet stirred up the thick clouds.

The collisions occurred over six days in July 1994. They hit the opposite side of the planet to Earth, but Jupiter's fast spin soon brought the impact site into view of *Galileo*. **Plumes** of gas rose thousands of miles (km) above the impact sites, allowing astronomers to study the chemicals in the clouds.

COULD HUMANS LIVE THERE?

One day the Jupiter system might be home to people, but it will not be an easy place to live.

MOON BASES

It is impossible to live on Jupiter itself, but humans could make a permanent base on one of the Galilean moons. There is a lot of ice around for making water, **oxygen**, and fuel, but the moons are dangerous places, with no air, freezing surfaces, and deadly **radiation** levels.

DANGEROUS ALIENS?

If space probes ever find traces of life in the Jupiter system, then a mission to collect samples would have to be very carefully planned. Contamination with alien germs, which evolved in a very different environment from Earth's, could kill the explorers. It might be safest for humans to keep our distance and send robots to investigate for us.

Astronomers have suggested the best place to build a Jupiter base would be in an ice crater on Callisto.

GLOSSARY

asteroid (AS-teh-royd) A large chunk of rock left over from when the planets formed.

atmosphere (AT-muh-sfeer) A layer of gas trapped by gravity around the surface of a planet.

atoms (A-temz) The smallest particles of a certain substance.

auroras (uh-ROR-uz) Colorful glows in the sky caused by charged particles hitting the atmosphere.

brown dwarf (BROWN DWAHRF) An object smaller than a star yet larger than a planet that produces light but not heat.

charged particles (CHARJD PAR-tih-kulz) Tiny pieces smaller than atoms or a small group of atoms that has an electric charge.

comet (KAH-mit) A large chunk of ice left over from when the planets formed. It develops a long, glowing tail of gas and dust as it nears the Sun.

core (KOR) The center of a planet or moon where the heaviest elements have collected.

craters (KRAY-turz) Holes made in the ground when a space rock smashes into a planet or moon.

crust (KRUST) The solid outer surface of a planet or moon, where the lighter elements have collected.

debris (duh-BREE) Pieces of rock, dust, ice, or other materials floating in space.

denser (DENTS-er) Having more weight squeezed into a small space.

element (EH-luh-ment) A chemical that cannot be split into another chemical. Hydrogen, helium, and iron are all examples of elements.

geyser (GY-zer) An eruption of scalding liquid and steam from under ground.

gravity (GRA-vih-tee) A force that pulls objects together. The heavier or closer an object is, the stronger its gravity.

helium (HEE-lee-um) The second-most-common element in the universe. Helium is one of the gases in Jupiter's atmosphere.

hemisphere (HEH-muh-sfeer) The top or bottom half of a planet, moon, or star.

hydrogen (HY-dreh-jen) The simplest, lightest, and most common element in the universe. Hydrogen is the fuel that makes stars shine. It makes up most of the gas in the Sun and in Jupiter.

magnetic field (mag-NEH-tik FEELD) The region around a planet where a compass can detect the north pole.

mantle (MAN-tul) The part of a planet or moon located between the core and the crust.

metallic hydrogen (meh-TA-lik HY-dreh-jen) Hydrogen atoms that are squeezed together so much that they begin to behave like a metal. They conduct electricity and are magnetic.

meteorites (MEE-tee-uh-ryts) Rocks from space that fall onto the surface of a planet or moon.

millenia (muh-LEH-nee-uh) Thousands of years.

mission (MIH-shun) An expedition to visit a certain place in space, such as a planet or moon.

molecules (MAH-lih-kyoolz) Tiny units of matter consisting of two or more atoms joined together.

NASA (NA-suh) The National Aeronautics and Space Administration, the U.S. space agency in charge of sending people and probes into space.

orbit (OR-bit) The path an object takes around another when it is trapped by the larger object's gravity.

oxygen (OK-sih-jen) The invisible gas in Earth's air that living things breathe in.

palimpsests (PA-lump-sests) The bright, frozen centers of large impact craters. They are made up of water and ice that welled up from inside the planet or moon.

plumes (PLOOMZ) Tall clouds of gas or smoke that rise high above the surrounding area.

pressure (PREH-shur) A measure of how much the air pushes down on you.

radiation (ray-dee-AY-shun) Energy let out in rays from a source, such as the Sun. Heat and light are types of radiation.

rotates (ROH-tayts) Turns around an object's central point, or axis.

poles (POHLZ) The top or bottom end of the axis of a planet, moon, or star.

probes (PROHBZ) Robotic vehicles sent from Earth to study the solar system.

solar system (SOH-ler SIS-tem) The planets, asteroids, and comets that orbit the Sun.

sulfur (SUL-fur) An element that has several different forms and colors.

temperature (TEM-pur-cher) How hot something is.

INDEX

WEB SITES

Due to the changing nature of Internet links, PowerKids Press has developed an online list of Web sites related to the subject of this book. This site is updated regularly. Please use this link to access the list:
www.powerkidslinks.com/dsol/jupiter/